A DAY IN MY MIND

wop8CD4.tmpoleObject0.bin

Penned by

Marcus Fairley

Forward

This book is nothing but a hobby of mine that transform into my passion. 20 years ago, 19-year-old me use to walk down the street talking to myself out loud. Some might think that was the sign of a crazy person but for me it was a way to release all the thoughts I had running through mind. So one day instead of me talking out loud I begin to write everything down which helped get stuff off my mind and not look crazy in the process. I would go home and read everything I wrote and do my best to transform everything that I jotted down into a poem. This is how poetry became a hobby of mine because it gave me a way to relieve any stress that I was feeling.

I was 31 years old when I met Stephan Clay. I was at work sitting in the break room talking to Stephan and he begin to tell me about how he hosts a spoken word event that was happening the first and third Friday of every month. I thought that was dope that he had a spoken word event that he hosted. I told him I write poems every now and then so I can clear my head. He asked if he could read some of the poems I wrote. After he read what I showed him he invited me out to do open mic. A few weeks later I went and got on stage to read one of my poems and the love I received felt absolutely amazing. A few weeks later he asked me to be a featured poet in a sweetest day event he was hosting. From the moment I accepted is invitation to be a feature poet in his show was the day this hobby of mine became a passion.

My goal with this book is to create and inspire new thoughts in people. I know I might not touch everyone but as long as my words touch just one person then my purpose for writing this book will be fulfilled. So as you go through these pages I am inviting you to spend a day in my mind as I share my thoughts and feelings with you. Thank you for your support I truly appreciate it because you didn't have to buy my book but you choose to buy my book.

I would like to give a special thank you to everyone who helped me on this project. I would to thank Rosemarie Wilson for doing an amazing job on editing the book for me. I would like to thank Frank Hall for bringing my vision to life with his cover design, Babiboipromotions is the truth. I would like to thank Angel Elizabeth for doing an amazing job on the pictures I used inside of the book, Angel J photography was highly professional and it was a pleasure to work with. I would like to thank Hollis Hall for her amazing advice, guidance, for helping me read and tweak this book she is the best aunt ever in life.I know I missed one or two people but know your contribution is appreciated and loved. These people helped me bring a dream of mine to reality so for them I am forever grateful.

Table of Contents

Poetry..1

The Way I Feel...3

Daddy's Girl..5

She Makes Me Feel......................................6

Love is a Word 7

All the Way Love.......................................9

Can I? 10

Earn It 11

When I Close My eyes 13

Peach Fuzz 15

Addicted 17

Wonder 19

Thief...20

Found 21

The Dream...24

Daydream..25

Dam!!!!!! 27

Untitled 29

My Vows...31

Couple of 4Evers......................................33

New Book..35

The Moment..37

Lost 39

A Love 41

I Tried 42

Left Unspoken 43

Shadow 45

Real Nigga 47

Tray 49

Questions from an Angel....................51

All the Way 54

Can't Lead...56

Molded Me 59

Poetry

Poetry is art.

Paper's my canvas.

The pen, my brush!

With these tools I create images only my soul has seen.

With each stroke,

the picture becomes clearer.

My Visions begins to jump off the page

making it impossible not to see through me.

Let me take your mind on a fantastic voyage.

Let's have a sit down with Mr. Rogers in his neighborhood.

Let's turn fiction into fact,

while I turn imagination into reality

with a functionary tale, becoming the facts of your life…

Over the years I have created pictures,

learning that poems do not actually have to rhyme,

they just need to contain passion in every line…

the shit that enlightens your soul

inspiring new thoughts in your mind.

I desire to write poems that will have the reader sitting on the
edges of their seats

biting their nails waiting on the next line.

I do this for the love of poetry

when I pick up my pen

writing from my heart

until my soul pours out.

The Way I Feel

Let me try to explain the way I feel.

Something is building up inside of me that I can no longer contain

nor can I control the emotions that have taken over my soul.

It feels like I am alone in my darkest hour.

Down on my knees,

As I look to the sky crying out for a higher power

to show me the way so I can accomplish what I dream of each night—

a good job,

crazy, sexy cool wife

and to be the father who makes his children proud.

I would defeat every monster hiding under my baby's beds,

make my woman feel like the most beautiful woman on earth.

I want to reach the highest heights

because I know favor is not fair

but someone must receive it,

why not me?

My heart and soul pour out onto the paper.

If I am judged for this,

I have no regrets.

I have enough faith to move mountains

while expressing how I feel.

God did not bring me this far to leave me.

If I keep the faith and stay prayed up,

There will never be a day he will not carry me through

to express the way, I feel.

Daddy's Girl

Daddy's Girl is the reason my heart beats,

my greatest inspiration,

the answer to my every prayer

and the greatest gift God has ever given.

I would sell every material possession that I own

to provide a better life for her

so that she can realize her dreams.

She can have the clothes off my back

and the last dime in my pocket.

She will always be the first lady in my life.

because nothing or no one comes before her.

I am proud of everything she accomplishes,

congratulating her every step of the way

as she approaches womanhood.

Although she still has a long way to go,

as long, as I have breath,

she will never walk alone.

I will always be there

ensuring she is in the best position to succeed.

She Makes Me Feel

She makes me feel like a soft teddy bear

even though I am hard

freaking

fracking

core.

I feel like her personal pillow

as I love to feel her head on my chest when she sleeps.

When she says "Da-Da" my heart melts

like a giant M&M.

She makes me feel things I never imagined I would feel.

She found buried treasure in my soul,

releasing emotions, I thought were hidden.

This love cannot be explained

but feels better than an 85-degree day in the middle of winter.

Whenever she cries,

I run to her.

She has got me wrapped around her little fingers.

I could go on for days telling you how she makes me feel,

but I am too hard core for all that mushy stuff.

Love is a Word

Love is a word that cannot be defined in a single line.

Unfortunately, most people will not be able to define love
within their lifetime.

Love is often misused or taken out of context

by boys upon girls for bodily exploration,

virginity taking

or emotional symbolization…

When a man uses the word love,

it symbolizes emotions that he cannot be describe.

After God made the object of his affection,

he broke the mold because

man did not deserve two women like Eve on this earth.

Most girls use love for monetary gain or materialistic
possessions.

When a woman utters the word love,

it is to symbolize a bond they want to last for a lifetime

with hopes of beginning a story better than any fairy tale
Disney ever produced.

But the irony about love is that it only cares about itself.

No two people will have the same meaning of this word

With communication,

trust, support, and understanding

two people can make a meaning of this word

together

to grow a bond too strong for any man to break

creating a love that will last forever

withstanding the tests of time.

All The Way Love

I want an all the way,

not a half-time

love

from someone who empowers me to be the best man I can possibly be.

Someone who will brighten my darkest hour,

encouraging me to achieve every goal I set.

I want an all the way love

who takes action without uttering

one

single

word.

Someone who will make two become one while we grow old

together

losing ourselves within a bond that time can't break.

I just want an all the way love

of

my

own.

Can I?

Can I be your rock?

No, no umm!!! I mean

that moon in your night sky?

Can my eyes be your light?

the stars that illuminate the darkest night.

Can I run your bath water?

prepare dinner with a tall glass of wine before we sit
down to unwind?

Can I assist in fulfilling your desires and needs?

I took cuts in line

so, you will not waste any time with those fake dudes
standing in line.

I am who you have been searching for

from the first time you opened your eyes,

took your first breath and let out that first cry.

I used to be the kind of man

who only wanted to bend you over,

smack your behind as I travel deep inside your happy
place.

Only to one night you.

Over time I have matured into a man

Who just wants to hold your hand,

forever.

I am ready to drop down on one knee to make an honest woman out of you.

I am the master key that will unlock the buried treasures

hidden deep within your heart,

if you will allow me to.

There are so many wonderful things I would love to do with and for you.

But before I do,

I just need to ask one question.

Can I?

Earn It

How can I earn it?

I mean,

How can I learn

you?

Do I need to work 18 hour shifts 7 days a week?

or do I need multi-millions saved in an offshore account?

Shall I prove my love by committing a crime, so you will know how down I am

for you?

I will travel to the ends of the solar system just to hear your voice,

to feel your touch...

I want to massage your mind to create new thoughts that send shocks down your spine.

I want you to have multiple braingasms

as I stimulate every part of you.

Must I let the world know what you mean to me?

I will support your hopes as I fuel your dreams.

I just want to stand beside you on your pedestal

so that the world can see me as your king, my queen.

What do I have to do to earn it?

Shit, it really does not matter what I have to do,

just know, there is nothing I would not do

to earn the right to call you mine

and hold you in my arms for a lifetime.

When I Close My Eyes

At night while I sleep,

there is not a moment I dream of being without you.

I love waking up with you lying in my arms

as we share every moment of our lives

as one.

I would rather not have my next breath

because I cannot breathe without you.

My heart cannot beat without you.

I am panic-stricken when I wake up without you.

My friends clown this love.

They are blind to it all from the outside looking in.

They give advice without due diligence

knowing not how you carried me

when I could not carry myself.

They did not see me in your arms

when tears would not stop flowing from my eyes…

You are the lifeguard who saved me from drowning in my
own sorrow...

You are the medicine I needed to make the pain go away.

Webster has no words to describe you,

because they do not exist.

The moment I looked into your eyes,

I saw my destiny.

You are what dreams are made of.

I am speechless until I close my eyes

then I come alive again when you lay in my arms.

Peach Fuzz

I am looking for something that is soft,

yet firm,

juicy and sweet...

something like a Georgia peach.

I need it to explode with flavor

when I place it on my tongue.

I want it to be so sweet to the point I get cavities,

filling my mouth until its juices escape the corners of my
mouth.

Truth is this drives me insane.

I cannot function, thinking about how good it is.

It had me sucking my thumb.

I put an A.P.B out on it,

but my body shook from flashbacks

when I went to the police—

I forgot how to speak

my mouth needs serious help

I hope she comes back to me

the reward will be absolute pleasure

from tongue tricks

she couldn't imagine

even if she tried.

Addicted

I love the treasure that resides in between her thighs.

I dig for gold,

diving into her ocean

headfirst

until I drown between her thighs.

This feeling intensifies each time I slide into her deep.

I take breaths,

exhale with pure ecstasy

there is a rush that pulls me in deeper.

I am addicted to her juices

like a fiend on the hunt for that rock...

I am searching for her kitty cat.

She purrs from my touch

then cries when my tongue runs circles around her G-spot.

That is the cat call I yearn for,

although this addiction may lead to my demise.

It has taken over me.

My thoughts are forever occupied with images of jumping

between her thighs

before she squirts into my eyes.

I am blinded by this addiction.

Only she can hear my cries.

Wonder

You are better than any word I could use describe such greatness.

God drew me a masterpiece,

beginning with your curves,

then your body began to take shape.

He penned your eyes perfectly for men to lose themselves,

gave you a smile brighter than the sun,

moon

and the stars

before he filled you with intelligence,

love

and a hint of loyalty.

You make angels jealous

because you are God's greatest creation gifted to man,

handcrafted

just

for

me.

Thief

You are looking at the greatest thief of all time

I stole a piece of heaven

for my benefit on earth—

an angel

straight from the hands of God

to stand by my side.

I found love the second we met.

She is the reason that I been able to overcome

any obstacle that I had to face.

Her life is now in my hands.

I promise to fulfill your wants,

needs

and every desire.

I will always love you

just the way you are,

even if your body changes

or you feel undesirable.

You are my blessing I took from Gods grip

for which I am thankful that he allowed me to keep.

Found

The moment I found you,

I discovered the meaning of true love.

You are the reason I stand tall today.

No matter what anyone may say,

don't ever change one thing for me.

I will always love you just the way you are.

My hands will shield you from harm.

They will ease your fears,

as I wipe your tears away.

I feel like a man holding his child for the first time

when you are in my arms.

I see light in your eyes

while tears form and fall from mine.

I want you spiritually,

not with your legs in the air

with your toes pointing to the sky.

Let me hold you tight as we make love from darkness into
the morning light.

I will lie beside you,

holding you tight

refusing to take my next breath if you leave my side.

I want to be with you for a lifetime.

I am talking white picket fence,

kids,

a big house

the whole nine.

I am happy you initially gave me a few moments of your time

so, I could convince you to be mine.

I want to be the man you long to see.

The brother you wake up to after you have had a good
night's sleep.

I strive to be anything and everything you need me to be.

I feel like a performer that has hit the stage for the first time
when I am in your presence.

My palms are sweaty—

My knees shake…

When I am done

I hope to receive the standing ovation

That our love deserves.

I am on a mission to travel to the depths of your soul.

to open the four chambers of your heart

replacing your blood with my love

allowing your heart to pump these feelings through your
veins.

I prepared your thoughts for a mind takeover

in hopes of capturing your spirit

so, I can touch every inch of your frame

with the love that radiates from within my soul for you.

The moment I found you

was the moment I found something better than my wildest
dreams

for you are my dream

come

true.

The Dream

I shared my dreams with you

letting you fulfill my every desire

before and after the storms raged.

You protected me from my fears

and the rain

empowering my imagination

leaving your heart within my safe space

for the creation of more dreams.

Marry me!!!

making two become one

then we will plant seeds which will multiply

us.

Feed the desire for me in your soul.

Keep me on the forefront of your mind.

I will never kill your dreams.

I am selling tickets that only you can cash.

Save them for a rainy day.

Continue to fight for us then I will see you later

in my dreams.

Daydream

I could not sleep last night.

Every time I closed my eyes,

the brightness of your smile shined behind my eyelids.

You have invaded my dreams,

corrupting my thoughts.

My mind is gone.

I can only shake my dam head as

I have not had a clear thought since the first time I saw your face.

I have no desire to rest.

I am afraid to blink my eyes

because that would mean I would have to go a moment

without

you.

Don't think I'm crazy.

I just don't want to miss any opportunity to be blessed by your presence.

you don't have a clue about how I feel for you

Teddy said it best--

you're my latest and greatest inspiration.

I have never met anyone like you.

Someone beautiful as well as kind,

who asks for nothing from me but to be myself.

Someone who lifts me up in prayer,

motivating me to achieve goals that I never knew was possible.

The best moments of my day are waking up beside you

then holding your entire body until you fall asleep

I cannot live without you by my side.

I am going to do everything within my power to show you,

That you are loved,

needed

and wanted

for a lifetime.

Dam!!!!!!!

I can't get her off my mind.

She was 5'10" with caramel skin

hazel brown eyes,

thick

with a big behind.

I keep having visions of her tongue running down my
shaft,

Diving off my barrel as she catches each shot, I shoot.

I see her sweet spot as my Hollister

I slide my fingers in my holster to find it is wetter than the
ocean.

She moaned which let me know she was enjoying the
moment

she asked if I was a plumber ready to lay that pipe.

I said "hell yeah"

the moment I put the tip in she closed her eyes as her
head fell back

she gently bit her bottom lip

I begin gyrating between her thighs then pulling out
slowly

so, I could watch her cream.

Each time I pulled the trigger she busts,

She was made just for me.

I fit perfectly and this feels so damned right.

I want to have her for life,

but these are just visions of a dream that I had last night.

Sculptor

I always wanted to hold you.

I consider you clay.

Let me mold you.

I would create a sculpture to honor you

so that the world would have no choice but to acknowledge
you.

Your greatness will reign from coast to coast,

like a cruise ship sailing across the ocean.

My feelings cannot be denied.

When you touch me,

my temperature starts to rise.

You have created a fire within my soul,

flames so intense that Superman couldn't extinguish

even if he blew with all his might.

Let me in.

To feel every inch of you,

As I sculpt,

hopefully, I'm creating feelings inside you that will be
impossible for you to

recreate even in your dreams.

Let this not be make believe.

Bob the Builder could not draw up the prefect blueprint

showing us how to build a love that will last until the day God tells us well done.

Today I am taking a stand,

starting by holding your hand.

I will share with you my deepest fears,

my darkest secrets

and every part of me.

You are the dream I pray to wake up to—

Every day I am allowed to open my eyes.

My Vows

The second I laid eyes on you,

I forgot how to speak.

My voice has been replaced with the words that I wrote.

At hello,

I felt like a baby who had never taken a step.

But you carried me,

caring for me when I didn't care about myself.

You showed me what the word love actually meant,

so, I vow on this day

to love you unconditionally…

to protect you from every danger you'll face in this lifetime…

to help you raise our children as strong individuals.

I vow to love you more than life itself

as I need you more than my next breath.

I will be your friend first—

the person you can talk to about anything.

Then I'll be the lover of your mind,

body,

and soul.

the co-pilot that flies with you to make your dreams become
reality.

I vow to help you solve every problem you face

asking God for mercy and his saving grace.

I pledge these vows and more to you,

eternally my love.

Amen.

Couple of 4evers

I thought we would raise our kids together

Showing them a love that lasted a couple of 4evers

I would want to tell them stories about the fourth of July
when our 4ever began

How I saw fireworks in your eyes

Felt the breeze flowing through the trees

We were gentle and ever so free

I thought I would sit them down then

Watch them grow

starting their own families

But we were never the couple who made

4ever...

My advice to the children I didn't have who seek a lifetime of
love

Stand together in unity

Speak words with compassion

If one falls, may the other pick them up

This is only the beginning of the best recipe

to make a couple of 4evers

last for an eternity

New Book

I just read a new book

only to find out you were the moral of the story.

I was intimidated by its length, so I judged the book by its cover

instead of taking time to enjoy the read.

I figured there would be treasures hidden in between the lines

but I was too lazy to finish,

blinded by selfish,

worldly desires.

I only saw what laid on the surface,

your breasts,

your ass

and the buried treasure that hides between your thighs.

I didn't notice your smile shining brighter than stars in a pitch-black sky.

I overlooked your brilliant mind,

the fact that you are more loyal than Jesus Christ with God.

Too many times I chased a new ass

becoming an ass

for not cultivating what was supposed to last 'til the end of

time...

a treasure bearing the gift between her thighs.

I refuse to miss out on forever again

because I was too lazy to read the pages

between the covers.

That is the only way to discover a woman's worth.

The Moment

The moment you left is the second you took my breath away.

Every minute without you,

I wanted to die by my own hand.

Hours turned into days,

days shifted into months where you weren't by my side,

but you would torture me by showing up in my dreams.

So many sleepless nights

I stared aimlessly out of the window…

Seasons changed

but my love remained the same.

One day I looked into the sky

only to see your smile in the sun

making me hotter than July.

Time is still ticking without you.

I realized there is no place like home

even though the grass did look greener on the other side.

At that moment,

I realized I needed you back in my life

Because I didn't appreciate what I had until it was gone.

My arms spread wide awaiting your return.

Let's not let years turn into decades before you return home.

I need you wrapped in my arms if only for a moment.

I will rock you to sleep,

holding you tight until morning when you wake still in my arms.

My first words will be blessed assurance that I will be better

today,

this afternoon

and in the evening

because I plan on spending the rest of my days with you...

'til the day my heart ceases to beat...

'til the day I'm called home to be judged by our Father.

Let us not play pretend.

Come home again

so, we can enjoy our moment

in a world that is our very own.

Lost

I can't believe this shit!

It happened to me twice.

I stand, looking in the mirror

watching tears fall from my eyes.

I can't help but wonder why,

why me?

I was supposed to be your shelter,

the person you came home to, to keep you safe at night.

I was supposed to be your protection from the rain.

the umbrella that kept you dry in the midst of every storm.

the crutch to hold you up

when you didn't have the strength to stand on your own...

I was the man that thought he had found his buried treasure

that hid beneath the sand since the beginning of time.

The moment I decided to give you the world

was the moment our present shattered

leaving our past in a billion pieces.

If you're willing,

we can rebuild for the future with shards from our broken
past

which will be better than either one of us could have ever
imagined.

Just like fairy tales,

every love story should have a happy ending.

Some people are placed in our lives for a season,

not a lifetime.

Green leaves wilt into brown

the same way love sometimes fades to black as love is blind

only caring about itself.

As tears fall from my eyes,

I still manage to smile

because even though all I see is darkness

a light will always shine through

as a reminder that brighter days are ahead.

A Love...

I want a love no one can see,

One that I'm afraid to possess,

that inspires me to overcome any obstacle.

I want to feel love deep within my soul

That sends shockwaves throughout my body

that causes sleepless nights.

I have had this before,

but now it is gone...

no longer lying by my side.

It slipped away due to pride.

I was wrong for not holding on to what was better than
anything I had ever imagined.

My deepest fantasy came true in my darkest hours

yet I searched for greener pastures in scorched grass.

The love I sought,

I already had.

Now I am looking for a new love

hoping I will be able to give

what I once received.

I Tried…

I tried to count every breath I took,

each step that I took today,

every beat of my heart,

how many times I blinked my eyes,

then I realized

I was blessed to even open my eyes.

I tried to count the sins which God forgave of mine

processing thoughts so I wouldn't repeat them

when he put someone new in my life.

I tried to make myself a better person

fighting battles on my own hoping for the victory,

self-medicating when I was sick.

Healing only came through Him,

my battles were already won.

I tried to live life alone,

but realized I am nothing without Him.

I can't live my way.

The Lord leads me.

I follow Him into greatness,

Accepting every blessings that He has in store for my life.

Left Unspoken

Some doors are best left unopened.

Just like some words are best left unspoken.

Those that will not uplift the soul

that break it down

to the point of non-existence.

They will have you picking up knives to slit your wrists

while blood drips from your veins

creating a puddle,

leaving stains on the brains of

every man,

woman,

and child who saw you

as their heart.

If you would only remember the words that took your eyes
off the prize…

the plan that God had for your life…

the reason why you're now seeing the light

as you stand before the Father awaiting his judgment.

He looks at you with tears in his eyes

before asking the question

Why?

Why did you take away the greatest gift I gave to man?

Why did you open the forbidden door?

My child,

I tried to save you from the evil that waits on the other side.

I locked the door then threw away the key.

The serpent deceived you

with promises of relieving the weights of the world

that kept you down.

You chose not to trust me,

thinking you knew what was best for your life.

If you had only followed my plan…

I can't allow you to enter the kingdom

for you have done the one thing that I cannot forgive.

I close the gates of heaven

because you have left words unspoken

misunderstanding why I locked a few doors.

As fire burns eternally,

I can no longer protect you from evil.

It no longer hides on the other side.

Shadow

I am standing outside on the concrete in the sunshine.

I looked back

and all I saw was my shadow.

Whenever the clouds took over the sky

and the storms came,

God was my anchor in the shadow

He held me down,

encouraging me to get up.

He promised that he would never leave me.

I feel stupid sometimes when I look back and I don't see him there.

I know he is guiding me through good and bad times.

holding my hand letting me know that everything is going to be alright.

He performed surgery on my soul time and time again,

painting a vivid picture of perfection as the sun shined through him,

healing whatever ailed my being.

You are leading me to the Promised Land.

I promise wherever you go,

I will follow without question.

Real Nigga

We have been enslaved since the beginning of time,

though some believe we have been set free.

Our bodies have been let go,

but our minds never left the plantation.

They are still tied down with chains

while master gives us our daily whippings,

calling us niggas,

still seeing us as merchandise

to be locked up under the guise of the highest bidder.

Young black children have taken over the job of the Klan

killing each other like animals at slaughter.

They use the word nigga

like it is the best word they have ever been introduced to

thinking the more they use it,

the connotation will become positive.

They get angry when the other brother uses niggas against
them

giving misdirected power to the vernacular that,

shows their true color—

ignorant.

We must realize that real niggas will create a shortage of
real men

leading to the extinction of black males as we know them.

I beg you,

young man

to become a strong

black man.

Respect yourself.

Respect others.

Lead your peers.

Teach them to be something

you never had a desire to become.

Tray

I lay on the ground with my head turned to the side

with tears falling from my eyes

because nobody answered my cries.

I was not the little boy crying wolf,

that title belonged to the shooter.

I didn't expect that the morning

I chose to wear a black hoodie,

tied my Jay's,

grabbed my cell

and started my day,

it would be the last time I saw the sun shine.

All I wanted was to remain dry in the storm,

a sweet tea to clinch my thirst

and Skittles to satisfy my sweet tooth.

The rain was actually God's tears

because he knew my time was up

and I would die at the hand of a racist.

I lay on the ground staring at the smoking gun.

All I could see was hate

then I wondered why it was my life he chose to take.

Was it the color of my skin?

The way I carried myself?

This damned hoodie.

Now I am gone but he's still roaming free.

I wanted to show the world that my life mattered.

But it doesn't matter,

now.

I am resting,

but not in peace

because my brothers and sisters

are still losing their lives

at the hand of racist sons of bitches

and we're no better off now

than we were 400 years ago

R.I.P. Trayvon Martin

Questions from an Angel

What's good with you bro?

Shit, just chilling…

I need to ask you a few serious questions.

What up doe?

What are your intentions with my girl and my son?

Don't you mean what are my intentions with my girl and your son?

Will you take care of them like they deserve to be taken care of?

Of course, I will.

How are you going to do this?

Fuck you mean, how?

Are you judging me from streets paved with gold?

Dude, you best calm down before the big fella kicks you out…

Just because you live in paradise

doesn't mean you made her feel like she was heaven sent.

Are you going to answer my question?

I'm going to treat her like she's the only woman left on the face of the earth;

honor her wishes and grant her desires;

treat her like the queen she is.

And, what about my son?

Don't you mean what about our son?

How is my son yours when I fertilized that egg?

You may have fertilized the seed,

but I have raised him since he was 6 months old.

I saw his first steps.

When he said Da-Da,

his first words,

they were directed at me.

I held his mother's hand when they put flowers on your head stone.

I don't take anything away from your memory.

I'm raising him with you.

How is that possible?

You are the angel who watches over him from above

I watch over him,

showering him with love.

Why should I believe you will always take care of them and be faithful to her?

Unlike you,

I don't play games.

I am positioned to be by her side until the end of time.

But I didn't play any games…

I can't understand how a lying,

cheating Devil became an Angel.

Play time is over.

I value my possessions.

I will be your guardian angel as long as you keep your word.

Thank you for looking out for us from behind the pearly gates.

I'm counting on you to raise our son to be the man I know he can be.

I thank God for this opportunity to kick it with you.

Remember we are both watching over you.

All The Way

I want to show you I will be here till the end of time

Be the solid foundation you build your life upon

Be the one who helps you accomplish your dreams when
even you don't believe it's

possible

The one you desire to see when you wake up in the morning
and lay beside when you go

to bed at night

I want you to feel comfortable to come to me about anything

The one you tell and talk to about everything

So if life ever beats you up I will be there to bandage your
wombs and nurse you back to

health

I will be the one on the days you feel like you can't make it to
carry you through

I just want to love you with everything that I have

So I pray to God you allow me to love you with every ounce
of energy that my soul possess

From this point forward we will be one mind, body, heart,
and soul

So by you choosing me means you have accepted all my
flaws

Accepted all my good and bad habits

You have overlooked my mistakes and decided to love me just the way I am

You choose to love me all the way

Just like I choose to love you with every single fiber of my being

So know there will never be a moment I love you less than all the way

Just like I pray there is never a second I don't show you that I do love you all the way

So if we stood on the highest mountain and you slipped off the cliff

Only for me to hold your life in my grip know I will never let you slip

Because without you I would be lost with no hope of being found

When I look into your eyes I see my destiny

That's how I know you were my gift from God

Can't Lead

Taking an eye for an eye creates blindness.

The blind cannot lead the blind,

neither will be able to see where they're going.

Two wrongs don't make one right.

Leading a horse to water doesn't mean it will drink.

in other words what I am saying just because you explain
something to someone doesn't mean they understand it
or is willing to take your advice

He politely stopped me and asked me what the hell I was
talking about awwwww!!! do you need a hug

shut up nigga lmao no I was just thinking and I can finally
see why a man who has all the money in the world can
be depressed

Or how a man feels that has four women and loses one
can be sad about it

this is because if you don't have the person you want to
share it with then everything else becomes meaningless

then this nigga going to say what woman done left you
and got you all in your feelings dam she done pussy
whipped your ass

I said shut up nigga you know ain't nobody pussy
whipping me shit I whip the pussy

(he laughs and begins to shake his head)

you have no clue how it feels shit so what I had a few
other women I was talking to hell I answered her calls
and did whatever she asked or needed me to do

I was there every day, I called her every day, and I was
there every birthday and holiday

she knows I love her more than words can express, why
did she have to leave me
I
(tears begin to fall from his eyes)

then going to tell me I cannot call, text, stop bye, or even
see her ever again

she knows I don't care about these other woman then
she going to call my ass selfish

saying you want to have your cake and eat it too she was
dead wrong

my friend stopped me again and gave me a hug then his
punk ass going tell me this

Dog I have known you forever and a day and you know I
will tell you when you're right and when you are wrong

So listen to me very carefully when I tell you this because
I am saying it out of love

you know you are wrong because if you thought she was
your pot of gold at the end of the rainbow you would of
did what was needed to obtain it

if you know the blind can't lead the blind you need to
open your eyes and listen to exactly what you are saying

it sounds like she took your ass to the water a countless amount of times but you just refused to drink thinking you knew a better way

So if you feel like you feel about her just let her go brother because you was wrong from the start and the wrong can't lead the right

just like two wrongs can't make a right cause if she continues to stay with you both of yal will be wrong

It's time for you to man up and if you love her you will do right by her and let her go so she can be happy and free

Molded me

You molded me into something I never knew I could be

You taught me the best things in life are free

I once thought the best things in life all had a price

I mean clothes, shoes, cars, houses, and hoes all have a price

But those worldly possessions couldn't compare to the treasure I found in you

See your touch sets my soul on fire

Which leaves a desire only you can fulfill

Your voice sounds like a melody from heaven

So I thank God for every moment he allowed me to have you in my life

I know every day hasn't been our best day

However, those days is why my love for you is stronger than the man of steal

You have earned my heart so I refuse to take it back

This mold you have made is one of a kind

Just like the love I have for you only comes once in a lifetime

You're my best friend the one I can talk to about anything

You're my shoulder to lean on when my legs are to weak
to hold me

You're my saving grace that gift from God that I thank
him for everyday

This is why I pray your will be in my life till the day God
calls us home